Religions of the World

Buddhism

Sue Penney

Heinemann
LIBRARY

www.heinemann.co.uk/library
Visit our website to find out more information about Heinemann Library books.

To order:
☎ Phone 44 (0) 1865 888066
▤ Send a fax to 44 (0) 1865 314091
▢ Visit the Heinemann Bookshop at www.heinemann.co.uk/library to browse our catalogue and order online.

First published in Great Britain by Heinemann Library
Halley Court, Jordan Hill, Oxford OX2 8EJ
a division of Reed Educational and Professional Publishing Ltd.
Heinemann is a registered trademark of Reed Educational & Professional Publishing Ltd.

OXFORD   MELBOURNE   AUCKLAND
JOHANNESBURG   BLANTYRE   GABORONE
IBADAN   PORTSMOUTH (NH) USA   CHICAGO

Designed by Ken Vail Graphic Design, Cambridge
Originated by Universal
Printed in Hong Kong by Wing King Tong.

ISBN 0 431 14953 4

06 05 04 03 02
10 9 8 7 6 5 4 3 2 1

J294.3
1305339

British Library Cataloguing in Publication Data
Penney, Sue
Buddhism. – (Religions of the world)
1. Buddhism – Juvenile literature
I. Title
294.3

Acknowledgements
The publishers would like to thank the following for permission to reproduce copyright material: All quotations are from *The Dhammapada*, Penguin Books, 1973 © Penguin Books Ltd 1973. Reproduced by permission of Penguin Books Ltd.

The Publishers would like to thank the following for permission to reproduce photographs: Andes Press Agency p. 38; Ann & Bury Peerless, pp. 13, 34; Associated Press p. 27; Carlos Reyes-Manzo, Andes Press Agency p.5; Circa Photo Library pp. 11, 15, 20, /William Holtby pp. 22, 25, 32, 39, /John Smith p. 23; Corbis p. 29; Hutchison Library, pp. 4, 7, 8, 10, 12, 18, 19, 24, 40, 42, /Carlos Freire p. 28, /Michael Macintyre pp. 30, 33; Impact pp.14, 37, /Mark Henley p. 26, /Dominic Sansoni p. 35; Phil & Val Emmett p. 6; Robin Bath pp. 17, 21, 31, 36, 41, 43.

Cover photograph reproduced with permission of E. T. Archive.

Our thanks to Philip Emmett for his comments in the preparation of this book.

Words appearing in the text in bold, **like this**, are explained in the Glossary.

Contents

Dates: In this book, dates are followed by the letters BCE (Before the Common Era) or CE (Common Era). This is instead of using BC (Before Christ) and AD (*Anno Domini* meaning In the year of our Lord), which is a Christian system. The date numbers are the same in both systems.

Introducing Buddhism

The teaching called Buddhism began in India about 2500 years ago. The teacher was a man called Siddattha Gotama. He lived in India in the sixth century BCE. Siddattha Gotama is called the **Buddha**, but this was not his name. It is a special title, which means someone who has gained **Enlightenment**. Enlightenment means being able to see things as they really are. (Think of turning on a light to see better.)

What do Buddhists believe?

Buddhists believe that the Buddha saw the truth about what the world is like. They believe that nothing in the world is perfect, and that the Buddha found the answer to why it is like this. They do not believe that the Buddha was a god. He was just a human being like them. They believe that he was important because he gained Enlightenment, and he chose to teach other people how to reach it, too.

Nibbana

Buddhists believe that there is a cycle of birth, life, death and rebirth. This goes on and on. They believe that unless someone gains Enlightenment, when they die they will be reborn. If a person can gain Enlightenment, they can break out of this cycle.

The lotus flower is often used by Buddhists to describe how people should live. It rises out of mud, but becomes a beautiful flower at the surface.

Breaking out of the cycle is called **Nibbana** (sometimes called Nirvana). It is the end of everything that is not perfect. It is perfect peace.

Meditation

Buddhists try to reach Nibbana by following the Buddha's teaching and by **meditation**. Meditation means training the mind to empty it of all thoughts. Then what is really important becomes clear.

Buddhists believe that by meditating they can become better people.

Buddhism fact check:

- *The teaching we call Buddhism began in India about 500 BCE.*
- *Buddhists follow the teachings of Siddattha Gotama, who is called the Buddha.*
- *Many Buddhists worship at home. They may also worship in temples.*
- *The most important teachings of Buddhism are called the Tipitaka, which means 'three baskets'.*
- *The symbol of Buddhism is a wheel with eight spokes. This reminds people that the Buddha taught about eight ways of living.*

The life of the Buddha

This tree in Sri Lanka grew from part of the original bodhi tree at Bodh Gaya.

The tree of wisdom

The bodhi tree means 'tree of wisdom'. Buddhists meditate at the bodhi tree at Bodh Gaya, because it is where the Buddha gained Enlightenment.

Siddattha's early life

Siddattha Gotama was born at Lumbini, in the country now called Nepal. His father was the local king. When Siddattha was born, wise men agreed that he would become a great leader. However, one of the wise men said that if Siddattha ever saw suffering, he would become the leader of a religion, not of a country. Siddattha's father wanted him to be the next king, so he ordered that no one who was sick or old should come near the palace. Siddattha was not allowed to leave the palace grounds.

Siddattha grew up in the palace. He married a beautiful girl and they had a son. When he was about 29 years old, Siddattha disobeyed his father's orders. He went horse-riding outside the grounds. While he was out, he saw an old man, and a sick man. Then he saw a funeral, with people crying. He had never seen anything like this before.

Next, Siddattha saw a holy man, who had given up everything but who was happy. The holy man spent his life trying to find the answers to the problem of suffering in the world. Siddattha decided that he must try to find the answers, too.

You can find the places mentioned in this book on the map on page 44.

Enlightenment

Siddattha left his palace that night, to begin his search. He tried many different ways. He went to great teachers, and spent years with holy men. He did not find the answers. At last, he sat down under a great tree at Bodh Gaya and **meditated**. Today, this tree is called the **bodhi tree**. As he meditated, Siddattha gained **Enlightenment**. This means that he understood why suffering happens and how it can be stopped.

After this, Siddattha was called the **Buddha**. Buddhist teaching says that, having gained Enlightenment, he could have left earth. Instead he chose to stay, and he spent the rest of his life teaching. He passed away at the age of 80 (Buddhists do not say he died). His body was **cremated** and the **ashes** buried in **thupas**.

This statue of the Buddha is in Sri Lanka.

The early days of Buddhism

Buddhists believe that there were **Buddhas** before Siddattha Gotama, and that there will be other Buddhas in the future. They believe that the teachings of Siddattha belong to the time that we live in now.

When the Buddha began teaching after his **Enlightenment**, a group of people became his followers. The first followers were a group of holy men. Siddattha had searched for Enlightenment with this group. Later, other people became interested, including the Buddha's own son, Rahula. For 45 years, the Buddha travelled all over India and nearby countries, teaching people about the best way to live.

Emperor Asoka (273–232 BCE)

After the Buddha had passed away, his followers carried on his teaching. An **Emperor** of India called Asoka heard the Buddha's teaching about looking after everything that is alive. Asoka had been a fighter all his life, and he became worried about the suffering he had caused. He became a Buddhist, and tried to rule India following the Buddha's teachings. Asoka helped people to learn more about Buddhism.

This is one of the pillars put up by the Emperor Asoka to remember the Buddha. It is in Delhi, the capital of India.

He ordered that stone pillars should be put up at places where important things had happened to the Buddha. The pillars had writing carved on them explaining why they were there. Some of these pillars still exist today.

The spread of Buddhism

As Buddhism spread from one country to another, people did not always think that the same teachings were important. Some people began to think more about one teaching than another. This is why today there are different groups of Buddhists. They all follow the teachings of the Buddha, but they do not all follow them in the same way. Customs are not the same in every country where there are Buddhists. This means that festivals and other celebrations may be quite different in different countries.

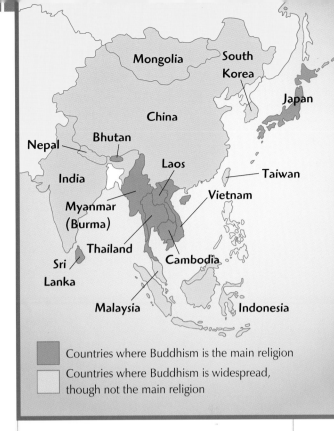

Countries where Buddhism is the main religion

Countries where Buddhism is widespread, though not the main religion

▲ *Countries in the world today where Buddhism is important.*

Buddhism today

The two main groups of Buddhists are Theravada Buddhists and Mahayana Buddhists. Buddhism is the main religion in Bhutan, Cambodia, Japan, Laos, Myanmar (Burma), Sri Lanka, Thailand and Vietnam. It is also important in other countries such as India, China and Malaysia. It is difficult to know exactly how many Buddhists there are in the world today, but the number is probably about 300 million.

The two main groups of Buddhists

You can find the places mentioned in this book on the map on page 44.

There are millions of Buddhists in the world. They all follow the teachings of the **Buddha**, but not all of them follow the teachings in the same way. There are groups with slightly different beliefs. In Buddhism, these groups are called 'schools'. There are two main schools of Buddhism.

Theravada Buddhists

One of the main schools of Buddhism is **Theravada** Buddhism. Theravada means 'teachings of the elders'. An elder is a leader of a religion – someone who is respected. Theravada Buddhism is sometimes called 'southern' Buddhism because most Theravada Buddhists live in Sri Lanka, Myanmar (Burma), Thailand, Cambodia and Vietnam.

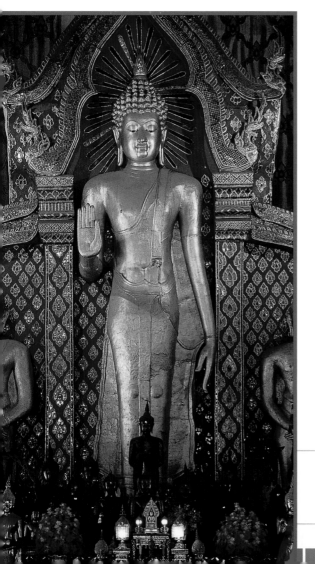

Theravada Buddhism teaches that every person must gain **Enlightenment** for themselves. The Buddha's teachings show people how to do this. Theravada Buddhists do not pray to the Buddha, because he was only a man. It is his teachings that can help people. Many Theravada Buddhists believe that the best way to live is as a **monk** or a **nun**. They believe that nuns and monks are closer to **Nibbana** than other people, because they do not have to think about a job, a family or running a home. Theravada Buddhists believe that it is their duty to give food and other gifts to nuns and monks.

A typical Theravada statue of Buddha looks calm and peaceful.

Mahayana Buddhism

The other main school of Buddhism is **Mahayana** Buddhism. Mahayana means 'great vehicle'. This is a way of saying that there are different ways of reaching Nibbana. Mahayana Buddhism has many groups, too. Some of these groups have changed the way that the teachings of Theravada Buddhism are explained. For example, Mahayana Buddhists think that, as well as many Buddhas, there have been many other people called **Bodhisattvas**, who can help them in their lives. They pray to them, and **meditate** to become more like them.

▲ *A typical Mahayana statue of Buddha is jolly and smiling.*

Mahayana Buddhism is most popular in the countries of China, Japan, Korea and Tibet.

The Three Jewels

Buddhists say that the most important parts of Buddhist belief can be summed up in the Three Jewels.

I take refuge in the Buddha
I take refuge in the Dhamma (teaching)
I take refuge in the Sangha (the Buddhist community).
(A refuge is a place where you are safe.)

Mahayana Buddhist groups

There are many different schools (groups) of Buddhism in **Mahayana** Buddhism. Some have many followers, while others have only a few.

These Zen Buddhist monks are meditating.

Zen Buddhism

Many followers of **Zen** Buddhism live in Japan. Zen is a Japanese word which means **meditation**. Zen Buddhists meditate for many hours each day. They call their meditation 'just sitting' or 'zazen'. The aim is to silence thoughts which are unhelpful. They call this 'training the mind'. Zen Buddhists believe that this will lead to **Enlightenment**. Zen Buddhists say that Enlightenment comes as a sudden flash of understanding. Zen Buddhist **monks** live in **monasteries**. They live very simple lives, often with strict rules about how they behave.

Pure Land Buddhism

Many followers of **Pure Land** Buddhism live in Japan. Pure Land Buddhists pray to a **Buddha** called Amida, who they believe is 'Lord of the Pure Land'. They say that the Pure Land is a place without suffering after this life, where it is easier to achieve **Nibbana**. Pure Land Buddhists believe that the Buddha Amida will help them to get there. Their special prayer is 'Nembutsu Amida', which means 'I call on you, Amida.' Prayers which are repeated over and over again, like this one, are called **mantras**.

Tibetan Buddhism

Tibetan Buddhists have great respect for a monk called the Dalai Lama. They believe that the Dalai Lama is an appearance of the **Bodhisattva** who is most special for the Tibetans. A Lama is a teacher or guide, and Tibetan Buddhists believe that the Dalai Lama can guide them to Enlightenment. When the Dalai Lama dies, a careful search is made for the person (usually a baby or young boy) who is believed to be the next appearance of the special Bodhisattva. After training to become a monk, he will be the next Dalai Lama.

Tibetan Buddhists write mantras and prayers on prayer wheels and flags. They believe that this is a way of making sure that the mantras are repeated over and over again. Repeating prayers like this is a way of getting **merit**. Merit is a reward for doing good things which helps a person on their way to Nibbana.

▲ *A prayer wheel in a Tibetan Buddhist monastery.*

Prayer wheels

A prayer wheel is a hollow cylinder filled with rolled-up paper which has mantras written on it. Some prayer wheels are quite small. Prayer wheels in temples may be so big that they need several people to push them.

What the Buddha taught

The **Buddha's** teaching is often divided into three parts. These are the Three Signs of Being, the Four Noble Truths and the Noble Eightfold Path.

The Three Signs of Being

The Three Signs of Being are ways that the Buddha used to describe life.

1. Nothing in life is perfect. This is described in the word **dukkha**. It includes things like being bored and uncomfortable, and everything which is not satisfactory.
2. Everything in life – even solid things such as mountains – is changing, all the time. This is described in the word **anicca**.
3. There is no **soul**. This is described in the word **anatta**. Instead, the Buddha taught, what does carry on to the next life is a person's life force (**kamma**). The kamma can be good or bad, depending on how the person lives in this life.

▲ *Buddhists believe that everyone should do their best, even though nothing in life is perfect.*

Buddhist teaching about the Noble Eightfold Path

Most people live as if they are walking across muddy ground. They can be helped only by people on firm ground. The Noble Eightfold Path helps to achieve this firm ground.

The Four Noble Truths

The Four Noble Truths explain more about the Buddha's teaching that everything is dukkha.

1. Everything is dukkha.
2. Dukkha is caused because everyone is greedy and selfish.
3. People can stop being greedy and selfish.
4. People can stop being greedy and selfish by following the Noble Eightfold Path.

This is Sarnath, where the Buddha first taught people about the Four Noble Truths.

The Noble Eightfold Path

The Noble Eightfold Path is the way that Buddhists should live their lives. The Buddha said that people should avoid extremes. They should not have or do too much, but neither should they have or do too little. The 'Middle Way' is the best. A Buddhist should try to follow all the parts of the Noble Eightfold Path at the same time. If Buddhists can do this, they can gain **Nibbana**. The eight parts of the Noble Eightfold Path are:

1. Right viewpoint (looking at things in the right way).
2. Right thought (using the mind in the right way).
3. Right speech (making sure that words do not hurt anyone).
4. Right action (not doing wrong things, as well as trying to do right ones).
5. Right living (not harming other people and doing a job which is useful).
6. Right effort (working hard to do good).
7. Right awareness (controlling the mind to look at things in the right way).
8. Right concentration (using meditation to help concentration).

Buddhist holy books

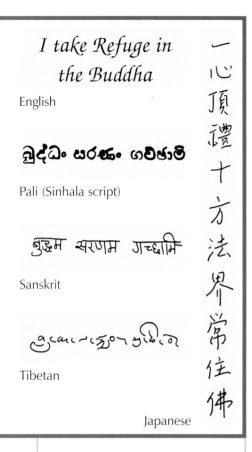

I take Refuge in the Buddha

English

 බුද්ධං සරණං ගච්ඡාමි

Pali (Sinhala script)

बुद्धम् सरणम् गच्छामि

Sanskrit

Tibetan

Japanese

一心頂禮十方法界常住佛

▲ *The Buddhist holy books are written in several different languages.*

After the Buddha

When the **Buddha** was alive, everyone remembered what he taught. When the Buddha passed away, there was a special meeting for 500 Buddhist **monks**. Two of the monks, who were the Buddha's closest friends, repeated all his teachings. All the monks agreed that the teaching was correct. For about 400 years, the teaching was passed down by monks. There were meetings at different times to check that everything was still being remembered correctly.

When the Buddha's teachings were finally written down, it was in two main collections. A collection of teaching is called a **canon**. The two Buddhist canons have the names of the languages in which they were first written. One is the **Pali** Canon. It is also called the **Tipitaka**. It is used by **Theravada** Buddhists. The other is the **Sanskrit** Canon, which is used by **Mahayana** Buddhists. The Pali Canon was written down first.

The Tipitaka

Tipitaka means three baskets. The Tipitaka was probably first written on palm leaves which were kept in three different baskets, so the Tipitaka has three parts, which are called 'baskets'. The first basket contains the rules which monks should follow, as well as some stories and other teachings. The second basket contains the teachings of the Buddha. The third basket contains writings which explain the Buddha's teachings.

Mahayana Buddhist holy books

Mahayana Buddhists also follow the teachings of the Tipitaka, but they do not agree with Theravada Buddhists about which teachings are the most important. For Mahayana Buddhists, two of the most important teachings are the Diamond **Sutra** and the Lotus Sutra. The Diamond Sutra was the first book in the world to be printed. Back-to-front letters carved on a block of wood were painted with ink and used as a stamp.

Mahayana Buddhists also believe that there were more teachings by the Buddha than those found in the Pali Canon, so these are included in the Sanskrit Canon.

▲ *Buddhist teachings are written on separate pieces of paper and kept in special boxes.*

Pali and Sanskrit

Pali and Sanskrit are very old languages. The Buddhist holy books were written down in both languages, so many Buddhist words can be spelled in two ways. For example, sutra is the Sanskrit form of the Pali word sutta.

What the holy books say

The most important Buddhist teachings are found in the **Tipitaka**, which means the three baskets. Most Buddhists agree on the teachings found in the first two baskets. **Mahayana** and **Theravada** Buddhists believe that different teachings should belong in the third basket.

▲ These **monks** are reading the holy books at a **monastery** in India.

The Buddha's last words

Just before he passed away, the Buddha said to his friends:

When I am gone, do not say that you have no teacher. Whatever I have taught, let that be your teacher when I am gone.

(Mahaparinibbana Sutta)

This helps to explain why Buddhists believe that the Buddha's teachings are so important.

The Sutta Pitaka

The most important of the three baskets is the **Sutta** Pitaka, because it contains the teachings of the **Buddha**. A sutta is a small piece of teaching. Part of this basket is called the Dhammapada. It contains some of the most important things that the Buddha said. Buddhists spend a lot of time studying these words. One part is more important than the others, because it is the Path of Teaching. This contains the Four Noble Truths and the Noble Eightfold Path. The Sutta Pitaka also contains stories about the Buddha. Some of the stories in the Sutta Pitaka, are about his other lives before he was Siddattha Gotama.

The Buddha's teaching

Much of the Buddha's teaching was about the importance of behaving in the right way. In the collection of his teachings called the Dhammapada, there are these words, which show how even the little things someone does may be important.

Hold not a sin of little worth, thinking 'this is little to me'. The falling of drops of water will in time fill a jar. Even so, the foolish man becomes full of evil, although he gather it little by little.

Hold not a deed of little worth, thinking 'this is little to me'. The falling of drops of water will in time fill a jar. Even so, the wise man becomes full of good, although he gather it little by little.
(Dhammapada 9: 121–2)

▲ This monk is praying at the feet of a statue of the Buddha in Thailand.

Symbols in Buddhism

A **symbol** is a sign. It is a way of showing something without using words. Using symbols means that complicated things can be made clear without a long explanation. Buddhists often use symbols in their worship, as well as to explain teaching and ideas.

Flowers

The lotus flower is often used as a symbol for Buddhism. It grows in the mud at the bottom of a pool, but rises above the surface to become a beautiful flower. Buddhists say that this is how people should rise above everything in life which is **dukkha**. Flowers are also a symbol of the Buddhist belief that everything is dukkha. A flower may be very beautiful and have a wonderful scent, but it soon withers and dies. This shows that nothing in life is perfect.

Candles

Candles are used as a symbol of the **Buddha's** teaching. Buddhists believe that what the Buddha taught can show them the way to live, just like a candle can bring light to a dark room.

The wheel of life

The symbol which is often used for Buddhism is a wheel with eight spokes. The eight spokes remind people about the Noble Eightfold Path. The wheel is also a reminder of the cycle of birth, death and rebirth.

*This statue shows the Buddha **meditating**. Notice the lotus flowers in the water.*

Statues of the Buddha

Statues of the Buddha include lots of symbols. There are 32 symbols in Buddhism which show that the Buddha was a special person. Any or all of these symbols can be used on statues. For example, the Buddha is often shown with a bump on the top of his head. This is a symbol that he had special talents. He is often seen with a round mark on his forehead, which is called the third eye. This is a symbol to show that he could see things ordinary people cannot see.

He may be shown with curled hair, which is a symbol that he was a very holy man. Sometimes he has long ears, which is a symbol that he came from an important family, and also that he could hear things that other people could not. People who understand these symbols know that they show the Buddha was very special.

▶ *A mandala is a pattern of shapes which some Buddhists use to help them to meditate.*

Mandalas

Mandala means circle. Mandalas are patterns made up of circles, triangles, squares and diamonds. They are usually made with coloured sand, though they can be stitched or painted. They are very important in Tibetan Buddhism. Some mandalas include pictures of the Buddha or a Bodhisattva.

How Buddhists worship

Some Buddhists do not like using the word worship, because in most religions worship means praying to God or gods. Buddhists do not do this. When it is used in this book, worship means the way Buddhists **meditate** and read the holy books.

Days of worship

There is no special day of the week when Buddhists worship. Days before the moon is new, full or at half-moon are important. Full-moon days are most important of all, because Buddhists believe that the **Buddha** was born, gained **Enlightenment** and passed away on days when the moon was full.

Worship alone

When Buddhists worship alone, they usually meditate and read from the Buddhist holy books. They may burn incense, which is a sweet-smelling perfume. They may offer small presents to a statue of the Buddha. These are often flowers or food like grains of rice. It is not the gift that is important, it is the love that it shows. Worship usually includes lighting candles, which are a **symbol** to show how the Buddha's teachings light up their lives. **Mahayana** Buddhists pray to **Bodhisattvas** as part of their worship.

*This shrine is in a **Tibetan** Buddhist's house in the UK.*

Worship in a group

Many Buddhists worship on their own. If they meet with others for worship, it is usually in a special building called a **temple**. The most important room in the temple contains the **shrine**. Inside the shrine is a statue of the Buddha. It is beautifully decorated with gold and lots of coloured patterns.

▲ *This statue is at Sarnath in India, where the Buddha taught for the first time.*

There are no seats in a shrine room. The people sit on the floor, or sometimes lie flat on the floor. They bow or put their hands together. These are ways of showing respect to the statue of the Buddha. Sometimes they touch their chest, lips and forehead with their hands, to show that all their body is joining in worship. People often offer gifts of flowers and incense, and light candles or small lamps. During worship, **monks** may read from the Buddhist holy books, and a senior monk may give a talk.

Meditation

When Buddhists meditate, they control their mind so they can concentrate on things that are really important. They become very calm. To meditate, Buddhists may focus on a statue of the Buddha or on another beautiful object. They believe that meditating will help them to gain Enlightenment.

Buddhist monks and nuns

These young monks are in the grounds of their monastery.

Buddhist **monks** and **nuns** live in the same way. However, there are many more monks than nuns. In this book, we will focus on monks.

Where do monks live?

Buddhist monks live in a **monastery**. Many monasteries have huts in the grounds where the monks live, eat and sleep. The huts have very simple furniture – a small table or stool, and a mat to sleep on. A monk does not own anything except the robes he wears, and necessary things like a bowl for food and a razor to shave his head. Anything else in the hut belongs to the monastery.

Monks may spend most of the day on their own, reading and **meditating**. There is usually a time when they study and meditate together. Some monks work as teachers, or help people in some other way. The **Buddha** taught that helping other people is important. All monks live very simply. They often eat only one meal a day, which is always before midday. After this they **fast** until the next day, though they are allowed to drink water.

Boys often become monks for just a few years, especially in **Theravada** Buddhist countries. Being in the monastery is like being at school. Any Buddhist man can become a monk. Many adults join the monastery for a few months or years, to learn more about Buddhism before they go back to their normal lives.

Alms

Monks are given food and everything they need by people who live near the monastery. This is called giving **alms**. It is not begging, because people are not asked to give.

Buddhism teaches that giving to others is important. Giving to the monks is especially important, because it is part of a Buddhist's duty. They also believe that it earns **merit** for the people who give. Merit is the reward for doing good things which helps people on thier way to **Nibbana**.

▲ *These Buddhist nuns come from Myanmar (Burma).*

Living as a monk

There are five **precepts** which all Buddhists follow. Buddhist monks and nuns follow these very strictly. There are also five more precepts which all monks and nuns are expected to follow. They agree that they will not eat after midday, attend music or dancing, use perfume or jewellery, sleep on a comfortable bed or accept gifts of money.

The Five Precepts

All Buddhists are expected to follow the Five Precepts. These are guides for living as a Buddhist. The Five Precepts are: not to harm anything which is alive; not to take anything which is not given; not to commit adultery; not to talk carelessly or unkindly; and not to drink alcohol or misuse drugs.

25

Two Buddhist temples

▲ *The Shwe Dagon Pagoda is an example of a thupa.*

You can find the places mentioned in this book on the map on page 44.

The Shwe Dagon Pagoda, Myanmar

The Shwe Dagon Pagoda in Rangoon is the oldest Buddhist **temple** in Myanmar (Burma). It is one of the most important Buddhist temples in the world. More than 2500 years ago, eight hairs from the **Buddha's** head were taken there. They have been kept there ever since.

The Shwe Dagon Pagoda is built in the shape of a **thupa**. The pagoda itself (the pointed section at the centre of the temple) is 100 metres high. In 1774 CE, the king of Burma ordered that the pagoda should be covered in gold. The amount of gold weighed the same as the king! The pagoda has 1500 bells. One hundred of them are made of gold, and the rest are made of silver. There are stairs and paths made of marble, with lots of **shrines** where Buddhists can worship. Every year thousands of people visit the Shwe Dagon Pagoda.

The Chuang Yen Monastery, USA

The Chuang Yen **Monastery** is just outside New York, USA. It is a monastery for **Pure Land** Buddhists. A group of **monks** and **nuns** live in the monastery. They spend their time teaching people about Buddhism.

The most important room is the Hall of Ten Thousand Buddhas. It contains a statue of the Buddha which is more than 11 metres high – higher than six men standing on each other's shoulders!

This is the largest statue of the Buddha in the Western world. It took eight years to build, and it is so large that the hall had to be built around it. Around the outside of the building is a wall painting which includes 10,000 small statues of the Buddha.

Another important room in the Chuang Yen Monastery is the Kuan Yin room. Kuan Yin is an important **Bodhisattva** for Pure Land Buddhists. The room contains two rare statues of Kuan Yin. One is made of china, and is almost 700 years old. The other is made of wood. It is almost two metres tall and may be more than 1000 years old.

▲ The statue of the Buddha at the Chuang Yen Monastery in the USA.

Thupas (also called Stupas)

Thupas are buildings or mounds of earth, which are usually built to the same pattern. There is a mound which is a symbol of earth, air, fire and water, and a tower which is a symbol of wisdom. The first thupas were places where the ashes of the Buddha were buried. Later, thupas were built where important Buddhists were buried.

Pilgrimage

A **pilgrimage** is a journey which people make because of their religion. Buddhist pilgrims may go to places where the **Buddha** lived or taught. They may also visit **thupas** where part of the Buddha's **ashes** were buried. They believe that going to these places will help them to gain **Enlightenment**.

Lumbini

You can find the places mentioned in this book on the map on page 44.

The Buddha was born at a place called Lumbini, in the country now called Nepal. It is quite a difficult place to get to. Some Buddhist **monks** live in Lumbini, and there are **temples** where people can **meditate**. At the Buddha's birthplace there is a stone which says: 'Here the Buddha was born.'

Bodh Gaya

Bodh Gaya is in India. This is the place where the Buddha gained Enlightenment. Buddhists go there from all over the world, and it is one of the most important places of pilgrimage. A **bodhi tree** grows there. Pilgrims walk around the bodhi tree, and sit under it to meditate. Close to the tree is a stone which Buddhists believe is the one which the Buddha sat on while he was meditating. There are many temples nearby.

Pilgrims lighting candles at Bodh Gaya, where the Buddha gained Enlightenment.

Sarnath

Sarnath is just north of Varanasi in India. It is where the Buddha taught people for the first time after he had gained Enlightenment. It is also one of the places where the Buddhist **Emperor** Asoka put up a pillar to show that the place is important for Buddhists. The top of this pillar has four lion heads, and it is now in the museum at Sarnath.

Other important places

There are many places in India and in other countries which Buddhists may visit on pilgrimage. For example, Sri Pada is a mountain in Sri Lanka. It is very important for Buddhists because they believe that the Buddha visited it. At the top of the mountain is a stone which has marks like footprints on it. Buddhists believe that these were made by the Buddha. Many Buddhists go on pilgrimage to watch the sun rise from the top of Sri Pada.

Sunrise over the top of Sri Pada, Sri Lanka.

The bodhi tree

More than 2000 years ago, the daughter of the Indian Emperor Asoka went to Sri Lanka to tell people about Buddhism. She took with her a branch from the bodhi tree at Bodh Gaya. It was planted, and grew. It still survives in the town of Anaradhapura in Sri Lanka. People believe that it is the oldest tree in the world.

Celebrations – Wesak and Hana Matsuri

Wesak

The most important Buddhist festival is held on the day of the full moon in May or June. **Theravada** Buddhists teach that on this very day, in different years, the **Buddha** was born, gained **Enlightenment** and passed away. The Wesak festival has different names in different countries, but it is celebrated by Buddhists all over the world.

In the UK and other Western countries, Wesak is often called Buddha Day. Buddhists go to a **temple** or **monastery**. They listen to a talk by the **monks** about the Buddha's life and his Enlightenment. They often repeat **mantras** and **meditate**. Many Buddhists give each other cards and presents.

Sharing a meal is an important part of the Buddha Day celebrations.

The Buddhist calendar

Buddhists follow a lunar year. This means that every month begins when there is a new moon, so each month lasts 29 or 30 days. Each Buddhist year is about 10 days shorter than a Western year. The most important days of the month for Buddhists are days when there is a full moon or a new moon.

In Sri Lanka, special ceremonies and worship take place in the temples at Wesak. There are huge lanterns in the streets and temples, with paintings on them showing scenes from the Buddha's life. There are plays and dancing. Everyone makes a special effort to be kind to others. This is to remind everyone what the Buddha taught.

In Thailand, the Wesak festival is called Vaisakha. People listen to monks giving talks about the life of the Buddha. The **shrines** in the temples are beautifully decorated. A special part of the festival is at night, when the statue of the Buddha is taken outside. People walk around it three times, carrying candles. They pour scented water over the statue. The statue is surrounded by light and sweet smells.

Hana Matsuri

Each year, **Mahayana** Buddhists celebrate the Buddha's birth in April, his Enlightenment in December and his passing away in February. In Japan, Mahayana Buddhists celebrate the birth of the Buddha with a flower festival called Hana Matsuri. People take offerings of spring flowers to decorate shrines and statues of the Buddha when he was a baby. People pour scented tea over the statues. This remembers the Buddha's birth, when stories say two streams of perfume from the sky bathed him and his mother.

As part of the celebrations of Hana Matsuri, people pour scented tea over statues of the Buddha.

Celebrations – Kathina and Songkran

Kathina

Kathina is a **Theravada** Buddhist festival. It is most important in Thailand, Sri Lanka and Myanmar (Burma). It takes place at the end of the rainy season. People take presents to the **monasteries** to say 'thank you' to the **monks** for all the work they do during the year.

Monks are not allowed to own anything themselves, so the presents are given to the monastery. The presents are usually cloth for new robes. The head of each monastery decides which monk or monks should be given a new robe.

These people are celebrating the festival of Kathina. They are taking cloth for robes to a Buddhist monastery.

Celebrating Buddhist festivals

Festivals are times to remember the Buddha's teaching. Not all Buddhists celebrate the same festivals, and celebrations may be different in different countries.

Buddhists believe that giving things at this time of year will earn **merit** for the giver. Merit is the reward for doing good things which helps a person to gain **Nibbana**.

Songkran

The festival of Songkran takes place in the month of April and lasts for three days. In Thailand, Songkran falls at the time of the New Year. People go to the monasteries, and give presents such as food and flowers to the monks. New Year is a chance to make a new start, so everyone wears new or clean clothes, houses are cleaned and rubbish is thrown away.

Water is very important in the festival of Songkran. There are often water fights on the streets, and boat races are held on the rivers. There is dancing and fireworks and people often watch shadow plays. These have a light shining behind a screen, and people making puppets move. The light makes big shadows of the puppets, which are then used to act out a story. Songkran ends when monks in the monasteries ring a bell and beat a huge drum. This is done three times, at midnight on the third day. When the sound has died away, the festival is over for another year.

Celebrations – Poson and Esala Perahera

The festivals of Poson and Esala **Perahera** are held in Sri Lanka.

Poson

Poson is the name of the month which falls in June/July in the Western calendar. The festival – also called Poson – is held on the day of the full moon. It celebrates the time when Buddhism was first brought to Sri Lanka in 250 BCE. Buddhists believe that in that year the king of Sri Lanka asked Emperor Asoka to send a **missionary** so that he could hear for himself the teachings of the Buddha. The Emperor sent his son, a Buddhist **monk** called the **Venerable** Mahinda. He preached to the king, who immediately became a Buddhist. The king then asked the Emperor to send an Order of Buddhist **nuns** and the Emperor sent his daughter, the Venerable Sanghamitta. She arrived with a branch of the **bodhi tree** in a golden vase. This was planted and it grew. The tree still survives, in the city of Anaradhapura, near the town of Mihintale. The **monastery** there is called the Shri Maha Bodhi, and is named after the tree.

You can find the places mentioned in this book on the map on page 44.

Each year, there are processions called **peraheras**, with huge floats. They carry statues that tell the story of Mahinda coming to Sri Lanka. The floats are surrounded by elephants wearing beautifully embroidered coats. Drummers follow the processions, and there are fireworks and dancing. The largest and most impressive processions are at Mihintale, the nearest town to where Mahinda first met the king.

The monastery at Shri Maha Bodhi is named after the tree (in the background in this photo) which grew from the branch brought by the Venerable Sanghamitta in 250 CE.

Esala Perahera

Esala Day is the day on which Buddhists all over the world celebrate the Buddha's first sermon. In Sri Lanka, Esala Day is a national holiday. One of the most impressive celebrations is held in the town of Kandy, in central Sri Lanka. A Buddhist temple there was specially built to keep a **relic** of the Buddha – one of his teeth. This is kept locked away in a special **casket**. For fifteen days every August the festival of Esala Perahera is held in its honour. The most important part of the festival is the perahera, a procession lit by torches, which takes place on the night of the full moon. Over 100 elephants take part in the procession. They are beautifully decorated, and wear brightly coloured cloths. The leading elephant carries a casket which is an exact copy of the one which holds the Buddha's tooth. (The real one is far too important to be taken out of the temple.) Other elephants carry caskets with relics of other important Buddhists. The procession travels through the town, watched by huge crowds.

Esala Perahera is a religious festival, but it is also a time for enjoying yourself, and there is a carnival on the streets. Dancers, drummers and fire-eaters accompany the procession, and people light fireworks and burn **incense** and other sweet-smelling perfumes.

Elephants and Buddhist festivals

Many Buddhist festivals use elephants as part of the celebrations. There are obvious reasons for this – Buddhism is at its strongest in countries where elephants have been used for centuries as beasts of burden and for transport. However, Buddhists also say that it is appropriate that they take part in festival processions because the Buddha once used the example of an elephant in his teaching. He pointed out that when a wild elephant is caught, it does not know how to behave and cannot be any use to its new master. In those days, in order to teach it what to do, elephant trainers would harness a wild elephant to a trusted tame one. The idea was that the tame one could teach the wild one. The Buddha advised his followers that they should do something similar in order to learn about Buddhism – they should find a Buddhist whom they trusted, and learn from him or her. Watching elephants in the festivals reminds Buddhists of this teaching.

These elephants are being prepared for a perahera.

Celebrations – some Mahayana Buddhist festivals

Losar

The festival of Losar is the New Year festival for **Tibetan** Buddhists. It begins at the full moon in February, and lasts for fifteen days. It is a time when people can make a fresh start. Homes and **temples** are cleaned and tidied. There are processions lit by torches, and special dances to scare away evil spirits.

The last day of Losar is called Changa Chopa. There are plays and puppet shows to describe events in the **Buddha's** life. Competitions are held to see who can make the best scenes. The amazing thing is that these scenes are made out of carved butter! Special dyes are used to make the butter look pretty, and wonderful patterns are made.

▲ *Carvings made from butter are part of the celebrations for Changa Chopa, the last day of Losar.*

Why are the bells rung 108 times?
Buddhist teaching says that 108 is the number of things that go wrong in people's lives. Examples are things such as greed, laziness and being jealous of others. Japanese Buddhists believe that every ring of the bells helps them to get rid of one of these faults.

New Year in Japan

New Year in Japan is 1 January. For Buddhists in Japan, the day before New Year is one of the most important days of the year. This is when the Evening Bells ceremony takes place. At midnight, the bells in every Buddhist temple in Japan are rung 108 times. As the bells ring, the people think about things that are wrong in their lives. They promise to try and do better in the year ahead.

Obon and Higan

Obon and Higan are both festivals when Buddhists in Japan remember people from their families who have died. The festival of Obon takes place in July. Buddhists in Japan believe that during Obon the **spirits** of people who have died come back to the family home. They light lamps to

These Buddhists in Japan are praying at a shrine on New Year's Eve.

show the spirits the way, and they put flowers on the family **shrine** to make it pretty for the spirits. **Mahayana** Buddhists believe that the Buddha can help people today, so they pray to the Buddha and ask his help for their relations.

The festival of Higan takes place twice a year, on days when the day and the night are the same length. At Higan, Buddhists in Japan clean and look after the graves of members of their family. They decorate them with flowers. They also hold special ceremonies which they believe can give **merit** to the people who have died. This is to help the people to gain **Nibbana**.

Special occasions – young people

There are only a few Buddhist celebrations for babies and young people. Most Buddhists follow the customs of the country in which they live. In different countries, Buddhists may celebrate in quite different ways.

The head shaving ceremony

In **Theravada** Buddhist countries, the main ceremonies for a baby happen when he or she is one month old. First, the baby's head is shaved. The **Buddha** taught that everyone has a life-force, called **kamma**, which carries on from one life to the next. Buddhists believe that the hair is a **symbol** of a bad kamma from a previous life, so they want to get rid of it. Then coloured threads are tied around the baby's wrists. The parents hope that these will bring good luck. The baby is often named at this ceremony. Sometimes **monks** are invited to this ceremony, and they may be asked to suggest the baby's name. The family always give food to the monks when a baby is born.

These boys are taking part in a ceremony to become ***Zen*** *Buddhist monks.*

Joining a monastery

Many Buddhist boys join a **monastery** for a short time. This may be only for a few months. In Myanmar (Burma) and Thailand, almost all boys join a monastery when they are about ten years old, so they can be taught by the monks.

In Myanmar, there is a special ceremony when a boy joins the monastery. It is called the pravrajya ceremony. The boy leaves his home, acting out the story of when Siddhattha Gotama left his royal palace and became a monk. When he gets to the monastery, the boy takes off his smart clothes. His head is shaved and older monks help him to dress in monk's robes.

▲ *A monk shaves a boy's head before the boy enters the monastery.*

He is given a new name, which he uses as long as he is a monk. Sometimes a boy's parents may give him presents such as a spare robe or the bowl he will need to collect his food.

The Buddha's teachings

The Buddha said that children are important. Parents should care for them. In return, children should respect their parents, and care for them in old age.

Special occasions – marriage and death

Marriage

Buddhist marriages usually follow the customs of the country. The parents of a young man or woman may suggest a person who would be suitable for them to marry. This is because marriage is so important and joins two families. **Astrologers** may be asked to suggest a good date for the wedding.

The marriage usually takes place in the bride's home. It is normally performed by a male relative of the bride. The couple stand on a platform called the **purowa**, which is decorated with white flowers. The couple usually give each other rings. The thumbs on their right hands are tied together, or their right wrists may be tied with a silk scarf. This shows they are being joined as husband and wife. Children read parts of the Buddhist holy books, and the couple promise to love and respect each other. Sometimes a **monk** gives a talk about the **Buddha's** teaching on marriage. At the end of the wedding, everyone shares a meal.

Buddhists in Hong Kong taking part in a wedding procession.

Death

Buddhists believe that death is not the end, because everyone who dies will be reborn. The funeral may be led by a monk who talks about the Buddha's teaching on what happens after death. Everyone repeats the Five **Precepts** and the Three Jewels, some of the most important things that Buddhists believe. In some countries, the body of a Buddhist who has died is **cremated**. In other countries, the body is buried.

When someone dies, their relations often give gifts to the monks. They ask that the **merit** gained by giving these gifts should be shared with the person who has died. They believe that this will improve their **kamma** and help them to gain **Nibbana**.

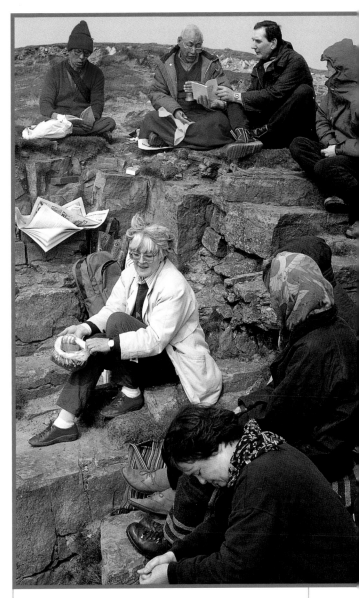

▲ *These Buddhists are taking part in a ceremony to remember a Buddhist **nun** who has died.*

Nibbana

The aim of all Buddhists is to gain Nibbana. Buddhists say that it is not really possible to describe what Nibbana is like. The word means going out, like a fire goes out because there is no fuel left. It is not life, and it is not death. 'You' no longer exist.

Ways to be a Buddhist

The Middle Way

The **Buddha** taught that the best way to live is the Middle Way, between extremes. This means that Buddhists do not choose to live in luxury or in a way that is very poor. Many Buddhists are **pacifists** who believe that it is wrong to fight.

Caring for others

Buddhists feel strongly that they are linked with other Buddhists in different countries. The word **Sangha** is very important. When the Buddha was alive, Sangha meant all Buddhists in all places. Today, it is usually used to mean Buddhist **monks** and **nuns**. **Mahayana** Buddhists use it to mean a group of Buddhists working together.

Buddhism teaches that family life is important, and that husbands and wives should respect and care for each other.

Giving to others – in this case to a monk – is an important part of Buddhist teaching.

Children should care for their parents and respect the memory of relatives who have died. Giving to others (**dana**) is very important, and Buddhists believe that it will earn **merit** for the person who is giving. The Buddha taught that the more someone gives, the less selfish they will become. Strangers should be welcomed and treated with respect and kindness.

Caring for the world

Buddhists in different countries live in very different ways, but Buddhism teaches that wherever they live, Buddhists should behave in a way that cares for others and the world around them. For example, many Buddhists would not work in jobs which involve making guns or other weapons, or selling alcohol or tobacco which can harm people's health.

In the past few years, ideas that Buddhists have been teaching for hundreds of years have become much more popular. Caring for the world is a very important Buddhist teaching. The world and everything in it should be treated carefully, so that people in years to come can enjoy the same things. Many other people are now also realizing that this is important. This is causing some people to become interested in Buddhism.

When Buddhists grow foods, they look after the land carefully. This farm is in Ladakh, in the Himalayan mountains.

A Tibetan Buddhist teaching

If I had not done harm to others,
No harm would come to me.
If I did harm living beings,
It is fit that harm returns to me.

Map

The globe on the right shows the location of the map below. The map shows places that are mentioned in this book. They are some of the places that are important in the history of Buddhism.

AFGHANISTAN

• Dharmsala

TIBET

H I M A L A Y A S

IRAN

R. Ganga

Kathmandu
•

CHINA

N

PAKISTAN

• Kushinara
NEPAL

Delhi •

• Lumbini

Varanasi •
BANGLADESH
Bodh Gaya •

0 _____ 1000 km
0 _____ 620 miles

INDIA

MYANMAR

LAOS

Rangoon •

THAILAND

Arabian Sea

Bay of Bengal

CAMBODIA

VIETNAM

Indian Ocean

• Anaradhapura
• Kandy
Sri Pada • •
• Mitintale
SRI LANKA

MALAYSIA

Place names

Some places on this map, or mentioned in the book, have been known by different names:

Sri Lanka – Ceylon   Myanmar – Burma   Varanasi – Benares

Timechart

Major events in World history

BCE	3000–1700	Indus valley civilization (Hinduism)
	c2685–1196	Egyptian civilization
	c2000	Abraham lived (Judaism)
	1800	Stonehenge completed
	c528	Siddhattha Buddha born (Buddhism)
	c450–146	Greek Empire
	200	Great Wall of China begun
	c300–300CE	Roman Empire
	c4	Jesus of Nazareth born (Christianity)
CE	570	Muhammad born (Islam)
	1066	Battle of Hastings and the Norman conquest of England
	1325–1521	Aztec Empire
	1400	Black Death kills one person in three in China, North Africa and Europe
	1469	Guru Nanak born (Sikhism)
	1564	William Shakespeare born
	1914–18	World War I
	1939–45	World War II
	1946	First computer invented
	1969	First moon landings
	2000	Millennium celebrations all over the world

Major events in Buddhist history

BCE	c563	Siddhattha Gotama born
	c528	Buddha achieves Enlightenment
	c483	Buddha passes away
	273–232	Emperor Asoka
	c200	Mahayana Buddhism begins
	c100	Holy books written down for the first time
CE	c100	Buddhism becomes popular in Tibet and Nepal
	c150	Ffirst Buddhist monastery in China
	c400	Huiyuan lives (began the Pure Land school)
	c500	Buddhism becomes popular in Korea
	868	Diamond Sutra printed in China (first ever printed book)
	c1100	King Anawratha lives (Burma)
	c1800	Buddhism spreads to America
	1893	First Buddhist missionary arrives in UK
	1959	Chinese invade Tibet – Dalai Lama goes to live in India

Glossary

adultery	sexual relations outside marriage
alms	giving food and necessary things to monks or nuns
anatta	belief that there is no soul
anicca	belief that nothing lasts and everything changes
ashes	the remains of a body left after cremation
astrologer	someone who studies the stars to tell the future
bodhi tree	tree under which the Buddha gained Enlightenment
Bodhisattva	someone who has chosen to be reborn, to help others gain Enlightenment
Buddha	one who has gained Enlightenment
canon	collection of teaching
cremate	burn a body after death
dana	giving to others
dhamma (or dharma)	the Buddha's teaching
dukkha	belief that nothing is satisfactory
Emperor	ruler of a country
Enlightenment	understanding the truth about the way things are
fast	do without food and drink for religious reasons
kamma (or karma)	force which a person creates during their life and which continues to their next life
Mahayana	school of Buddhism
mandala	special pattern
mantra	word or words repeated as a prayer
meditation	controlling your mind so that you can empty it of all thoughts

merit	reward for doing good things
missionary	someone who travels to tell people about his or her beliefs
monastery	place where monks live
monk	man who has dedicated his life to religion
Nibbana or Nirvana	'going out' – the end of things not being perfect
nun	woman who has dedicated her life to religion
pacifist	person who believes that disagreements should be solved without fighting
Pali	very old language
perahera	procession which is part of a festival
pilgrimage	journey made because of religion
precept	guide for living
Pure Land	school of Buddhism
purowa	platform on which a bride and groom stand to be married
Sangha	Buddhist community (today it means Buddhist monks and nuns)
Sanskrit	very old language
shrine	special place for worship
soul	part of a person's spirit
spirit	part of a person that lives on after death
sutta or sutra	small piece of teaching
symbol	sign which shows something
temple	place of worship
Theravada	school of Buddhism
thupa (or stupa)	burial mound where important Buddhist remains are buried
Tibetan	school of Buddhism
Tipitaka	'three baskets' – most important Buddhist teachings
Zen	school of Buddhism

Index

Titles in the *Religions of the World* series include:

Hardback   0 431 14953 4

Hardback   0 431 14950 X

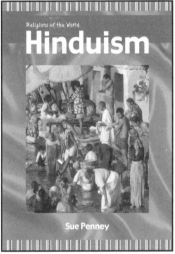

Hardback   0 431 14955 0

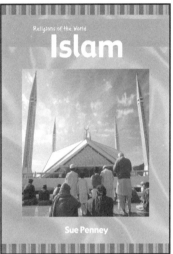

Hardback   0 431 14952 6

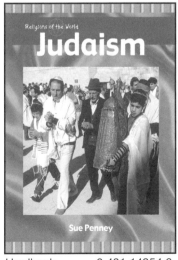

Hardback   0 431 14954 2

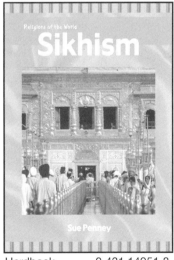

Hardback   0 431 14951 8

Find out about the other titles in this series on our website www.heinemann.co.uk/library